A Narrative of the Most Remarkable Particulars in the Life of James Albert Ukawsaw Gronniosaw

James Albert Ukawsaw Gronniosaw

A

NARRATIVE

OF THE

MOST REMARKABLE PARTICULARS

IN THE LIFE OF

JAMES ALBERT UKAWSAW GRONNIOSAW,

AN AFRICAN PRINCE,

As related by HIMSELF.

I will bring the Blind by a Way that they know not, I will lead them in Paths that they have not known: I will make Darkness Light before them and crooked Things straight. These Things will I do unto them and not forsake them. Isa. xlii. 16.

1772

TO THE

RIGHT HONOURABLE

The *Countess* of HUNTINGDON;

THIS

NARRATIVE

Of my *LIFE*,

And of GOD'S wonderful Dealings with me, is,

(*Through Her LADYSHIP'S Permission*)

Most Humbly Dedicated,

By her LADYSHIP'S

Most obliged

And obedient Servant,

JAMES ALBERT.

THE PREFACE to the READER.

THIS Account of the Life and spiritual Experience of JAMES ALBERT was taken from his own Mouth and committed to Paper by the elegant Pen of a young LADY of the Town of LEOMINSTER, for her own private Satisfaction, and without any Intention at first that it should be made public. But she has now been prevail'd on to commit it to the Press, both with a view to serve ALBERT and his distressed Family, who have the sole Profits arising from the Sale of it; and likewise as it is apprehended, this little History contains Matter well worthy the Notice and Attention of every Christian Reader.

Perhaps we have here in some Degree a Solution of that Question that has perplex'd the Minds of so many serious Persons, viz. In what Manner will God deal with those benighted Parts of the World where the Gospel of Jesus Christ hath never reach'd? Now it appears from the Experience of this remarkable Person, that God does not save without the Knowledge of the Truth; but, with Respect to those whom he hath fore-known, though born under every outward Disadvantage, and in Regions of the grossest Darkness and Ignorance, he most amazingly acts upon and influences their Minds, and in the Course of wisely and most wonderfully appointed Providences, he brings them to the Means of spiritual Information, gradually opens to their View the Light of his Truth, and gives them full Possession and Enjoyment of the inestimable Blessings of his Gospel. Who can doubt but that the Suggestion so forcibly press'd upon the Mind of ALBERT (when a Boy) that there was a Being superior to the Sun, Moon, and Stars (the Objects of African Idolatry) came from the Father of Lights, and was, with Respect to him, the First-Fruit of the Display of Gospel-Glory? His long and perilous Journey to the Coast of Guinea, where he was sold for a Slave, and so brought into a Christian Land; shall we consider this as the alone Effect of a curious and inquisitive Disposition? Shall we in accounting for it refer to nothing higher than mere Chance and accidental Circumstances? Whatever Infidels and Deists may think; I trust the Christian Reader will easily discern an All-wise and Omnipotent Appointment and Direction in these Movements. He belong'd to the Redeemer of lost Sinners; he was the Purchase of his Cross; and therefore the Lord undertook to bring him by a Way that he knew not, out of Darkness into his marvellous Light, that he might lead him to a saving Heart-Acquaintance and Union with the triune God in Christ reconciling the World unto himself; and not imputing their Trespasses. As his Call was very extraordinary, so there are certain Particulars exceedingly remarkable in his Experience. God has put singular Honour upon him in the Exercise of his Faith and Patience, which in the most distressing and pitiable Trials and Calamities have been found to the Praise and Glory of God. How deeply must it affect a tender Heart, not only to be reduc'd to the last Extremity himself, but to have his Wife and Children perishing for Want before his Eyes! Yet his Faith did not fail him; he put his Trust in the Lord, and he was delivered. And at this Instant, though born in an exalted Station of Life, and now under the Pressure of various afflicting Providences, I am persuaded (for I know the Man) he would rather embrace the Dung-hill, having Christ in his Heart, than give up his spiritual Possessions and Enjoyment, to fill the Throne of Princes. It perhaps may not be amiss to observe that JAMES ALBERT left his native Country, (as near as I can guess from certain Circumstances) when he was about 15 Years old. He now appears to be turn'd of Sixty; has a good natural Understanding; is well acquainted with the Scriptures, and the Things of God, has an amiable and tender Disposition, and his Character can be well attested not only at Kidderminster, the Place of his Residence but likewise by many creditable Persons in London and other Places. Reader, recommending this Narrative to your perusal, and him who is the Subject of it to your charitable Regard,

I am your faithful and obedient Servant,

For Christ's Sake,

W. Shirley.

AN

ACCOUNT

OF

JAMES ALBERT, &c.

I was born in the city BOURNOU; my mother was the eldest daughter of the reigning King there, of which BOURNOU is the chief city. I was the youngest of six children, and particularly loved by my mother, and my grand-father almost doated on me.

I had, from my infancy, a curious turn of mind; was more grave and reserved in my disposition than either of my brothers and sisters. I often teazed them with questions they could not answer: for which reason they disliked me, as they supposed that I was either foolish, or insane. 'Twas certain that I was, at times, very unhappy in myself: it being strongly impressed on my mind that there was some GREAT MAN of power which resided above the sun, moon and stars, the objects of our worship. My dear indulgent mother would bear more with me than any of my friends beside.—I often raised my hand to heaven, and asked her who lived there? was much dissatisfied when she told me the sun, moon and stars, being persuaded, in my own mind, that there must be some SUPERIOR POWER.—I was frequently lost in wonder at the works of the Creation: was afraid and uneasy and restless, but could not tell for what. I wanted to be informed of things that no person could tell me; and was always dissatisfied.—These wonderful impressions begun in my childhood, and followed me continually 'till I left my parents, which affords me matter of admiration and thankfulness.

To this moment I grew more and more uneasy every day, in so much that one saturday, (which is the day on which we keep our sabbath) I laboured under anxieties and fears that cannot be expressed; and, what is more extraordinary, I could not give a reason for it.—I rose, as our custom is, about three o'clock, (as we are oblig'd to be at our place of worship an hour before the sun rise) we say nothing in our worship, but continue on our knees with our hands held up, observing a strict silence 'till the sun is at a certain height, which I suppose to be about 10 or 11 o'clock in England: when, at a certain sign made by the priest, we get up (our duty being over) and disperse to our different houses.—Our place of meeting is under a large palm tree; we divide ourselves into many congregations; as it is impossible for the same tree to cover the inhabitants of the whole City, though they are extremely large, high and majestic; the beauty and usefulness of them are not to be described; they supply the inhabitants of the country with meat, drink and clothes;[A] the body of the palm tree is very large; at a certain season of the year they tap it, and bring vessels to receive the wine, of which they draw great quantities, the quality of which is very delicious: the leaves of this tree are of a silky nature; they are large and soft; when they are dried and pulled to pieces it has much the same appearance as the English flax, and the inhabitants of BOURNOU manufacture it for cloathing &c. This tree likewise produces a plant or substance which has the appearance of a cabbage, and very like it, in taste almost the same: it grows between the branches. Also the palm tree produces a nut, something like a cocoa, which contains a kernel, in which is a large quantity of milk, very pleasant to the taste: the shell is of a hard substance, and of a very beautiful appearance, and serves for basons, bowls, &c.

[A] It is a generally received opinion, in *England*, that the natives of *Africa* go entirely unclothed; but this supposition is very unjust: they have a kind of dress so as to appear decent, though it is very slight and thin.

I hope this digression will be forgiven.—I was going to observe that after the duty of our Sabbath was over (on the day in which I was more distressed and afflicted than ever) we were all on our way home as usual, when a remarkable black cloud arose and covered the sun; then followed very heavy rain and thunder more dreadful than ever I had heard: the heav'ns roared, and the earth trembled at it: I was highly affected and cast down; in so much that I wept sadly, and could not follow my relations and friends home.—I was obliged to stop and felt as if my legs were tied, they seemed to shake under me: so I stood still, being in great fear of the MAN of POWER that I was persuaded in myself, lived above. One of my young companions (who entertained a particular friendship for me and I for him) came back to see for me: he asked me why I stood still in such very hard rain? I only said to him that my legs were weak, and I could not come faster: he was much affected to see me cry, and took me by the hand, and said he would lead me home, which he did. My mother was greatly alarmed at my tarrying out in such terrible weather; she asked me many questions, such as what I did so for, and if I was well? My dear mother says I, pray tell me who is the great MAN of POWER that makes the thunder? She said, there was no power but the sun, moon and stars;

that they made all our country.—I then enquired how all our people came? She answered me, from one another; and so carried me to many generations back.— Then says I, who made the *First Man*? and who made the first Cow, and the first Lyon, and where does the fly come from, as no one can make him? My mother seemed in great trouble; she was apprehensive that my senses were impaired, or that I was foolish. My father came in, and seeing her in grief asked the cause, but when she related our conversation to him, he was exceedingly angry with me, and told me he would punish me severely if ever I was so troublesome again; so that I resolved never to say any thing more to him. But I grew very unhappy in myself; my relations and acquaintance endeavoured by all the means they could think on, to divert me, by taking me to ride upon goats, (which is much the custom of our country) and to shoot with a bow and arrow; but I experienced no satisfaction at all in any of these things; nor could I be easy by any means whatever: my parents were very unhappy to see me so dejected and melancholy.

About this time there came a merchant from the *Gold Coast* (the third city in GUINEA) he traded with the inhabitants of our country in ivory &c. he took great notice of my unhappy situation, and enquired into the cause; he expressed vast concern for me, and said, if my parents would part with me for a little while, and let him take me home with him, it would be of more service to me than any thing they could do for me.—He told me that if I would go with him I should see houses with wings to them walk upon the water, and should also see the white folks; and that he had many sons of my age, which should be my companions; and he added to all this that he would bring me safe back again soon.—I was highly pleased with the account of this strange place, and was very desirous of going.—I seemed sensible of a secret impulse upon my mind which I could not resist that seemed to tell me I must go. When my dear mother saw that I was willing to leave them, she spoke to my father and grandfather and the rest of my relations, who all agreed that I should accompany the merchant to the Gold Coast. I was the more willing as my brothers and sisters despised me, and looked on me with contempt on the account of my unhappy disposition; and even my servants slighted me, and disregarded all I said to them. I had one sister who was always exceeding fond of me, and I loved her entirely; her name was LOGWY, she was quite white, and fair, with fine light hair though my father and mother were black.—I was truly concerned to leave my beloved sister, and she cry'd most sadly to part with me, wringing her hands, and discovered every sign of grief that can be imagined. Indeed if I could have known when I left my friends and country that I should never return to them again my misery on that occasion would have been inexpressible. All my relations were sorry to part with me; my dear mother came with me upon a camel more than three hundred miles, the first of our journey lay chiefly through woods: at night we secured ourselves from the wild beasts by making fires all around us; we and our camels kept within the circle, or we must have been torn to pieces by the Lyons, and other wild creatures, that roared terribly as soon as night came on, and continued to do so 'till morning.—There can be little said in favour of the country through which we passed; only a valley of marble that we came through which is unspeakably beautiful.—On each side of this valley are exceedingly high and almost inaccessible mountains—Some of these pieces of marble are of prodigious length and breadth but of different sizes and colour, and shaped in a variety of forms, in a wonderful manner.—It is most of it veined with gold mixed with striking and beautiful colours; so that when the sun darts upon it, it is as pleasing a sight as can be imagined.—The merchant that brought me from BOURNOU, was in partnership with another gentleman who accompanied us; he was very unwilling that he should take me from home, as, he said, he foresaw many difficulties that would attend my going with them.—He endeavoured to prevail on the merchant to throw me into a very deep pit that was in the valley, but he refused to listen to him, and said, he was resolved to take care of me: but the other was greatly dissatisfied; and when we came to a river, which we were obliged to pass through, he purpos'd throwing me in and drowning me; but the Merchant would not consent to it, so that I was preserv'd.

We travel'd 'till about four o'clock every day, and then began to make preparations for night, by cutting down large quantities of wood, to make fires to preserve us from the wild beasts.—I had a very unhappy and discontented journey, being in continual fear that the people I was with would murder me. I often reflected with extreme regret on the kind friends I had left, and the idea of my dear mother frequently drew tears from my eyes.—I cannot recollect how long we were in going from BOURNOU to the GOLD COAST; but as there is no shipping nearer to BOURNOU than that City, it was tedious in travelling so far by land, being upwards of a thousand miles.—I was heartily rejoic'd when we arriv'd at the end of our journey: I now vainly imagin'd that all my troubles and inquietudes would terminate here; but could I have looked into futurity, I should have perceiv'd that I had much more to suffer than I had before experienc'd, and that they had as yet but barely commenc'd.

I was now more than a thousand miles from home, without a friend or any means to procure one. Soon after I came to the merchant's house I heard the drums beat remarkably loud, and the trumpets blow—the persons accustom'd to this employ, are oblig'd to go upon a very high structure appointed for that purpose, that the sound might be heard at a great distance: They are higher than the steeples are in England. I was mightily pleas'd with sounds so entirely new to me, and was very inquisitive to know the cause of this rejoicing, and ask'd many questions concerning it: I was answer'd that it was meant as a compliment to me, because I was Grandson to the King of BOURNOU.

This account gave me a secret pleasure; but I was not suffer'd long to enjoy this satisfaction, for in the evening of the same day, two of the merchant's sons (boys about my own age) came running to me, and told me, that the next day I was to die, for the King intended to behead me.—I reply'd that I was sure it could not be true, for that I came there to play with them, and to see houses walk upon the water with wings to them, and the white folks; but I was soon inform'd that their King imagined that I was sent by my father as a spy, and would make such discoveries at my return home that would enable them to make war with the greater advantage to ourselves; and for these reasons he had resolved I should never return to my native country.—When I heard this I suffered misery that cannot be described.—I wished a thousand times that I had never left my friends and country.—But still the ALMIGHTY was pleased to work miracles for me.

The morning I was to die, I was washed and all my gold ornaments made bright and shining, and then carried to the palace, where the King was to behead me himself (as is the custom of the place).—He was seated upon a throne at the top of an exceeding large yard, or court, which you must go through to enter the palace, it is as wide and spacious as a large field in England.—I had a lane of lifeguards to go through.—I guessed it to be about three hundred paces.

I was conducted by my friend, the merchant, about half way up; then he durst proceed no further: I went up to the KING alone—I went with an undaunted courage, and it pleased GOD to melt the heart of the King, who sat with his scymitar in his hand ready to behead me; yet, being himself so affected, he dropped it out of his hand, and took me upon his knee and wept over me. I put my right hand round his neck, and prest him to my heart.—He sat me down and blest me; and added that he would not kill me, and that I should not go home, but be sold, for a slave, so then I was conducted back again to the merchant's house.

The next day he took me on board a French brig; but the Captain did not chuse to buy me: he said I was too small; so the merchant took me home with him again.

The partner, whom I have spoken of as my enemy, was very angry to see me return, and again purposed putting an end to my life; for he represented to the other, that I should bring them into troubles and difficulties, and that I was so little that no person would buy me.

The merchant's resolution began to waver, and I was indeed afraid that I should be put to death: but however he said he would try me once more.

A few days after a Dutch ship came into the harbour, and they carried me on board, in hopes that the Captain would purchase me.—As they went, I heard them agree, that, if they could not sell me *then*, they would throw me overboard.—I was in extreme agonies when I heard this; and as soon as ever I saw the Dutch Captain, I ran to him, and put my arms round him, and said, "father, save me." (for I knew that if he did not buy me, I should be treated very ill, or, possibly, murdered) And though he did not understand my language, yet it pleased the ALMIGHTY to influence him in my behalf, and he bought me *for two yards of check*, which is of more value *there*, than in England.

When I left my dear mother I had a large quantity of gold about me, as is the custom of our country, it was made into rings, and they were linked into one another, and formed into a kind of chain, and so put round my neck, and arms and legs, and a large piece hanging at one ear almost in the shape of a pear. I found all this troublesome, and was glad when my new Master took it from me—I was now washed, and clothed in the Dutch or English manner.—My master grew very fond of me, and I loved him exceedingly. I watched every look, was always ready when he wanted me, and endeavoured to convince him, by every action, that my only pleasure was to serve him well.—I have since thought that he must have been a serious man. His actions corresponded very well with such a character.—He used to read prayers in public to the ship's crew every Sabbath day; and when first I saw him read, I was never so surprised in my whole life as when I saw the book talk to my master; for I thought it did, as I observed him to look upon it, and move his lips.—I wished it would do so to me.—As soon as my master had done reading I follow'd him to the place where he put the book, being mightily delighted with it, and when nobody saw me, I open'd it and put my ear down close upon it, in great hope that it wou'd say something to me; but was very sorry and greatly disappointed when I found it would not speak, this thought immediately presented itself to me, that every body and every thing despis'd me because I was black.

I was exceedingly sea-sick at first; but when I became more accustom'd to the sea, it wore off.—My master's ship was bound for Barbadoes. When we came there, he thought fit to speak of me to several gentlemen of his acquaintance, and one of them exprest a particular desire to see me.—He had a great mind to buy me; but the Captain could not immediately be prevail'd on to part with me; but however, as the gentleman seem'd very solicitous, he at length let me go, and I was sold for fifty dollars (*four and sixpenny-pieces in English*). My new master's name was Vanhorn, a young Gentleman; his home was in New-England in the City of New-York; to which place he took me with him. He dress'd me in his livery, and was very good to me. My chief business was to wait at table, and tea, and clean knives, and I had a very easy place; but the servants us'd to curse and swear surprizingly; which I learnt faster than any thing, 'twas almost the first English I could speak. If any of them affronted me, I was sure to call upon God to damn them immediately; but I was broke of it all at once, occasioned by the correction of an old black servant that liv'd in the family—One day I had just clean'd the knives for dinner, when one of the maids took one to cut bread and butter with; I was very angry with her, and called upon God to damn her; when this old black man told me I must not say so. I ask'd him why? He replied there was a wicked man call'd the Devil, that liv'd in hell, and would take all that said these words, and put them in the fire and burn them.—This terrified me greatly, and I was entirely broke of swearing.—Soon after this, as I was placing the china for tea, my mistress came into the room just as the maid had been cleaning it; the girl had unfortunately sprinkled the wainscot with the mop; at which my mistress was angry; the girl very foolishly answer'd her again, which made her worse, and she call'd upon God to damn her.—I was vastly concern'd to hear this, as she was a fine young lady, and very good to me, insomuch that I could not help speaking to her, "Madam, says I, you must not say so," Why, says she? Because there is a black man call'd the Devil that lives in hell, and he will put you in the fire and burn you, and I shall be very sorry for that. Who told you this replied my lady? Old Ned, says I. Very well was all her answer; but she told my master of it, and he order'd that old Ned should be tyed up and whipp'd, and was never suffer'd to come into the kitchen with the rest of the servants afterwards.—My mistress was not angry with me, but rather diverted with my simplicity and, by way of talk, She repeated what I had said, to many of her acquaintance that visited her; among the rest, Mr. Freelandhouse, a very gracious, good Minister, heard it, and he took a great deal of notice of me, and desired my master to part with me to him. He would not hear of it at first, but, being greatly persuaded, he let me go, and Mr. Freelandhouse gave £50. for me.—He took me home with him, and made me kneel down, and put my two hands together, and pray'd for me, and every night and morning he did the same.—I could not make out what it was for, nor the meaning of it, nor what they spoke to when they talk'd—I thought it comical, but I lik'd it very well.—After I had been a little while with my new master I grew more familiar, and ask'd him the meaning of prayer: (I could hardly speak english to be understood) he took great pains with me, and made me understand that he pray'd to God, who liv'd in Heaven; that He was my Father and BEST Friend.—I told him that this must be a mistake; that *my* father liv'd at BOURNOU, and I wanted very much to see him, and likewise my dear mother, and sister, and I wish'd he would be so good as to send me home to them; and I added, all I could think of to induce him to convey me back. I appeared in great trouble, and my good master was so much affected that the tears ran down his face. He told me that God was a GREAT and GOOD SPIRIT, that He created all the world, and every person and thing in it, in Ethiopia, Africa, and America, and every where. I was delighted when I heard this: There, says I, I always thought so when I liv'd at home! Now if I had wings like an Eagle I would fly to tell my dear mother that God is greater than the sun, moon, and stars; and that they were made by Him.

I was exceedingly pleas'd with this information of my master's, because it corresponded so well with my own opinion; I thought now if I could but get home, I should be wiser than all my country-folks, my grandfather, or father, or mother, or any of them—But though I was somewhat enlighten'd by this information of my master's, yet, I had no other knowledge of God but that He was a GOOD SPIRIT, and created every body, and every thing—I never was sensible in myself, nor had any one ever told me, that He would punish the wicked, and love the just. I was only glad that I had been told there was a God because I had always thought so.

My dear kind master grew very fond of me, as was his Lady; she put me to School, but I was uneasy at that, and did not like to go; but my master and mistress requested me to learn in the gentlest terms, and persuaded me to attend my school without any anger at all; that, at last, I came to like it better, and learnt to read pretty well. My schoolmaster was a good man, his name was Vanosdore, and very indulgent to me.—I was in this state when, one Sunday, I heard my master preach from these words out of the Revelations, chap. i. v. 7. *"Behold, He cometh in the clouds and every eye shall see him and they that pierc'd Him."* These words affected me excessively; I was in great agonies because I thought my master directed them to me only; and, I fancied, that he observ'd me with unusual earnestness—I was farther confirm'd in this belief as I look'd round the church, and could see no one person beside myself in such grief and distress as I was; I began to think that my master hated me, and was very desirous to go home, to my own country; for I thought that if God did come (as he said) He would be sure to be most angry with *me*, as I did not know what He was, nor had ever heard of him before.

I went home in great trouble, but said nothing to any body.—I was somewhat afraid of my master; I thought he disliked me.—The next text I heard him preach from was, Heb. xii. 14. *"follow peace with all men, and holiness, without which no man shall see the LORD."* he preached the law so severely, that it made me tremble.—he said, that GOD would judge the whole world; ETHIOPIA,

ASIA, and AFRICA, and every where.—I was now excessively perplexed, and undetermined what to do; as I had now reason to believe my situation would be equally bad to go, as to stay.—I kept these thoughts to myself, and said nothing to any person whatever.

I should have complained to my good mistress of this great trouble of mind, but she had been a little strange to me for several days before this happened, occasioned by a story told of me by one of the maids. The servants were all jealous, and envied me the regard, and favour shewn me by my master and mistress; and the Devil being always ready, and diligent in wickedness, had influenced this girl, to make a lye on me.—This happened about hay-harvest, and one day when I was unloading the waggon to put the hay into the barn, she watched an opportunity, in my absence, to take the fork out of the stick, and hide it: when I came again to my work, and could not find it, I was a good deal vexed, but I concluded it was dropt somewhere among the hay; so I went and bought another with my own money: when the girl saw that I had another, she was so malicious that she told my mistress I was very unfaithful, and not the person she took me for; and that she knew, I had, without my master's permission, order'd many things in his name, that he must pay for; and as a proof of my carelessness produc'd the fork she had taken out of the stick, and said, she had found it out of doors—My Lady, not knowing the truth of these things, was a little shy to me, till she mention'd it, and then I soon cleared myself, and convinc'd her that these accusations were false.

I continued in a most unhappy state for many days. My good mistress insisted on knowing what was the matter. When I made known my situation she gave me John Bunyan on the holy war, to read; I found his experience similar to my own, which gave me reason to suppose he must be a bad man; as I was convinc'd of my own corrupt nature, and the misery of my own heart: and as he acknowledg'd that he was likewise in the same condition, I experienc'd no relief at all in reading his work, but rather the reverse.—I took the book to my lady, and inform'd her I did not like it at all, it was concerning a wicked man as bad as myself; and I did not chuse to read it, and I desir'd her to give me another, wrote by a better man that was holy and without sin.—She assur'd me that John Bunyan was a good man, but she could not convince me; I thought him to be too much like myself to be upright, as his experience seem'd to answer with my own.

I am very sensible that nothing but the great power and unspeakable mercies of the Lord could relieve my soul from the heavy burden it laboured under at that time.— A few days after my master gave me Baxter's *Call to the unconverted*. This was no relief to me neither; on the contrary it occasioned as much distress in me as the other had before done, *as it* invited all to come to *Christ* and I found myself so wicked and miserable that I could not come—This consideration threw me into agonies that cannot be described; insomuch that I even attempted to put an end to my life—I took one of the large case-knives, and went into the stable with an intent to destroy myself; and as I endeavoured with all my strength to force the knife into my side, it bent double. I was instantly struck with horror at the thought of my own rashness, and my conscience told me that had I succeeded in this attempt I should probably have gone to hell.

I could find no relief, nor the least shadow of comfort; the extreme distress of my mind so affected my health that I continued very ill for three Days, and Nights; and would admit of no means to be taken for my recovery, though my lady was very kind, and sent many things to me; but I rejected every means of relief and wished to die—I would not go into my own bed, but lay in the stable upon straw—I felt all the horrors of a troubled conscience, so hard to be born, and saw all the vengeance of God ready to overtake me—I was sensible that there was no way for me to be saved unless I came to *Christ*, and I could not come to Him: I thought that it was impossible He should receive such a sinner as me.

The last night that I continued in this place, in the midst of my distress these words were brought home upon my mind, *"Behold the Lamb of God."* I was something comforted at this, and began to grow easier and wished for day that I might find these words in my bible—I rose very early the following morning, and went to my school-master, Mr. Vanosdore, and communicated the situation of my mind to him; he was greatly rejoiced to find me enquiring the way to Zion, and blessed the Lord who had worked so wonderfully for me a poor heathen.—I was more familiar with this good gentleman than with my master, or any other person; and found myself more at liberty to talk to him: he encouraged me greatly, and prayed with me frequently, and I was always benefited by his discourse.

About a quarter of a mile from my Master's house stood a large remarkably fine Oak-tree, in the midst of a wood; I often used to be employed there in cutting down trees, (a work I was very fond of) I seldom failed going to this place every day; sometimes twice a day if I could be spared. It was the highest pleasure I ever experienced to set under this Oak; for there I used to pour out all my complaints to the LORD: and when I had any particular grievance I used to go there, and talk to the tree, and tell my sorrows, as if it had been to a friend.

Here I often lamented my own wicked heart, and undone state; and found more comfort and consolation than I ever was sensible of before.—Whenever I was treated with ridicule or contempt, I used to come here and find peace. I now began to relish the book my Master gave me, Baxter's *Call to the unconverted*, and took great delight in it. I was always glad to be employ'd in cutting wood, 'twas a great part of my business, and I follow'd it with delight, as I was then quite alone and my heart lifted up to GOD, and I was enabled to pray continually; and blessed for ever be his Holy Name, he faithfully answer'd my prayers. I can never be thankful enough to Almighty GOD for the many comfortable opportunities I experienced there.

It is possible the circumstance I am going to relate will not gain credit with many; but this I know, that the joy and comfort it conveyed to me, cannot be expressed and only conceived by those who have experienced the like.

I was one day in a most delightful frame of mind; my heart so overflowed with love and gratitude to the Author of all my comforts.—I was so drawn out of myself, and so fill'd and awed by the Presence of God that I saw (or thought I saw) light inexpressible dart down from heaven upon me, and shone around me for the space of a minute.—I continued on my knees, and joy unspeakable took possession of my soul.—The peace and serenity which filled my mind after this was wonderful, and cannot be told.—I would not have changed situations, or been any one but myself for the whole world. I blest God for my poverty, that I had no worldly riches or grandeur to draw my heart from Him. I wish'd at that time, if it had been possible for me, to have continued on that spot for ever. I felt an unwillingness in myself to have any thing more to do with the world, or to mix with society again. I seemed to possess a full assurance that my sins were forgiven me. I went home all my way rejoicing, and this text of scripture came full upon my mind. *"And I will make an everlasting covenant with them, that I will not turn away from them, to do them good; but I will put my fear in their hearts that they shall not depart from me."* The first opportunity that presented itself, I went to my old school-master, and made known to him the happy state of my soul who joined with me in praise to God for his mercy to me the vilest of sinners.—I was now perfectly easy, and had hardly a wish to make beyond what I possess'd, when my temporal comforts were all blasted by the death of my dear and worthy Master Mr. Freelandhouse, who was taken from this world rather suddenly: he had but a short illness, and died of a fever. I held his hand in mine when he departed; he told me he had given me my freedom. I was at liberty to go where I would.—He added that he had always pray'd for me and hop'd I should be kept unto the end. My master left me by his will ten pounds, and my freedom.

I found that if he had lived 'twas his intention to take me with him to Holland, as he had often mention'd me to some friends of his there that were desirous to see me; but I chose to continue with my Mistress who was as good to me as if she had been my mother.

The loss of Mr. Freelandhouse distress'd me greatly, but I was render'd still more unhappy by the clouded and perplex'd situation of my mind; the great enemy of my soul being ready to torment me, would present my own misery to me in such striking light, and distress me with doubts, fears, and such a deep sense of my own unworthiness, that after all the comfort and encouragement I had received, I was often tempted to believe I should be a Cast-away at last.—The more I saw of the Beauty and Glory of God, the more I was humbled under a sense of my own vileness. I often repair'd to my old place of prayer; I seldom came away without consolation. One day this Scripture was wonderfully apply'd to my mind, *"And ye are compleat in Him which is the Head of all principalities and power."*—The Lord was pleas'd to comfort me by the application of many gracious promises at times when I was ready to sink under my troubles. *"Wherefore He is able also to save them to the uttermost that come unto God by Him seeing He ever liveth to make intercession for them. Hebrews x. ver. 14. For by one offering He hath perfected for ever them that are sanctified."*

My kind, indulgent Mistress liv'd but two years after my Master. Her death was a great affliction to me. She left five sons, all gracious young men, and Ministers of the Gospel.—I continued with them all, one after another, till they died; they liv'd but four years after their parents. When it pleased God to take them to Himself, I was left quite destitute, without a friend in the world. But I who had so often experienced the Goodness of GOD, trusted in Him to do what He pleased with me.—In this helpless condition I went in the wood to prayer as usual; and tho' the snow was a considerable height, I was not sensible of cold, or any other inconveniency.—At times indeed when I saw the world frowning round me, I was tempted to think that the LORD had forsaken me. I found great relief from the contemplation of these words in Isaiah xlix. v. 16. *"Behold I have graven thee on the palms of my hands; thy walls are continually before me."* And very many comfortable promises were sweetly applied to me. The lxxxix. Psalm and 34th verse, *"My covenant will I not break nor alter the thing that is gone out of my lips."* Hebrews, chap. xvi. v. 17, 18. Phillipians, chap. i. v. 6; and several more.

As I had now lost all my dear and valued friends every place in the world was alike to me. I had for a great while entertain'd a desire to come to ENGLAND.—I imagined that all the Inhabitants of this Island were *Holy*; because all those that had visited my Master from thence were good, (Mr. Whitefield was his particular friend) and the authors of the books that had been given me were all English. But above all places in the world I wish'd to see Kidderminster, for I could not but think that on the spot where Mr. Baxter had liv'd, and preach'd, the people must be all *Righteous*.

The situation of my affairs requir'd that I should tarry a little longer in NEW-YORK, as I was something in debt, and was embarrass'd how to pay it.—About this time a young Gentleman that was a particular acquaintance of one of my young Master's, pretended to be a friend to me, and promis'd to pay my debts, which was three pounds; and he assur'd me he would never expect the money again.—But, in less than a month, he came and demanded it; and when I assur'd him I had nothing to pay, he threatened to sell me.—Though I knew he had no right to do that, yet as I had no friend in the world to go to, it alarm'd me greatly.—At length he purpos'd my going a Privateering, that I might by these means, be enabled to pay him, to which I agreed.—Our Captain's name was —— I went in Character of Cook to him.— Near St. Domingo we came up to five French ships, Merchant-men.—We had a very smart engagement that continued from eight in the morning till three in the afternoon; when victory declar'd on our side.—Soon after this we were met by three English ships which join'd us, and that encourag'd us to attack a fleet of 36 Ships.—We boarded the three first and then follow'd the others; and had the same success with twelve; but the rest escap'd us.—There was a great deal of blood shed, and I was near death several times, but the LORD preserv'd me.

I met with many enemies, and much persecution, among the sailors; one of them was particularly unkind to me, and studied ways to vex and teaze me.—I can't help mentioning one circumstance that hurt me more than all the rest, which was, that he snatched a book out of my hand that I was very fond of, and used frequently to amuse myself with, and threw it into the sea.—But what is remarkable he was the first that was killed in our engagement.—I don't pretend to say that this happen'd because he was not my friend: but I thought 'twas a very awful Providence to see how the enemies of the LORD are cut off.

Our Captain was a cruel hard-hearted man. I was excessively sorry for the prisoners we took in general; but the pitiable case of one young Gentleman grieved me to the heart.—He appear'd very amiable; was strikingly handsome. Our Captain took four thousand pounds from him; but that did not satisfy him, as he imagin'd he was possess'd of more, and had somewhere conceal'd it, so that the Captain threatened him with death, at which he appear'd in the deepest distress, and took the buckles out of his shoes, and untied his hair, which was very fine, and long; and in which several very valuable rings were fasten'd. He came into the Cabbin to me, and in the most obliging terms imaginable ask'd for something to eat and drink; which when I gave him, he was so thankful and pretty in his manner that my heart bled for him; and I heartily wish'd that I could have spoken in any language in which the ship's crew would not have understood me; that I might have let him know his danger; for I heard the Captain say he was resolv'd upon his death; and he put his barbarous design into execution, for he took him on shore with one of the sailors, and there they shot him.

This circumstance affected me exceedingly, I could not put him out of my mind a long while.—When we return'd to NEW-YORK the Captain divided the prize-money among us, that we had taken. When I was call'd upon to receive my part, I waited upon Mr. — —, (the Gentleman that paid my debt and was the occasion of my going abroad) to know if he chose to go with me to receive my money or if I should bring him what I owed.—He chose to go with me; and when the Captain laid my money on the table ('twas an hundred and thirty-five pounds) I desir'd Mr. — — to take what I was indebted to him; and he swept it all into his handkerchief, and would never be prevail'd on to give a farthing of money, nor any thing at all beside.—And he likewise secur'd a hogshead of sugar which was my due from the same ship. The Captain was very angry with him for this piece of cruelty to me, as was every other person that heard it.—But I have reason to believe (as he was one of the Principal Merchants in the city) that he transacted business for him and on that account did not chuse to quarrel with him.

At this time a very worthy Gentleman, a Wine Merchant, his name Dunscum, took me under his protection, and would have recovered my money for me if I had chose it; but I told him to let it alone; that I wou'd rather be quiet.—I believed that it would not prosper with him, and so it happen'd, for by a series of losses and misfortunes he became poor, and was soon after drowned, as he was on a party of pleasure.—The vessel was driven out to sea, and struck against a rock by which means every soul perished.

I was very much distress'd when I heard it, and felt greatly for his family who were reduc'd to very low circumstances.—I never knew how to set a proper value on money. If I had but a little meat and drink to supply the present necessaries of life, I never wish'd for more; and when I had any I always gave it if ever I saw an object in distress. If it was not for my dear Wife and Children I should pay as little regard to money now as I did at that time.—I continu'd some time with Mr. Dunscum as his servant; he was very kind to me.—But I had a vast inclination to visit ENGLAND, and wish'd continually that it would please Providence to make a clear way for me to see this Island. I entertain'd a notion that if I could get to ENGLAND I should never more experience either cruelty or ingratitude, so that I was very desirous to get among Christians. I knew Mr. Whitefield very well.—I had heard him preach often at NEW-YORK. In this disposition I listed in the twenty-eighth Regiment of Foot, who were design'd for

The Life of James Albert Ukawsaw Gronniosaw

Martinico in the late war.—We went in Admiral Pocock's fleet from NEW-YORK to Barbadoes; from thence to Martinico.—When that was taken we proceeded to the Havannah, and took that place likewise.—There I got discharged.

I was then worth about thirty pounds, but I never regarded money in the least, nor would I tarry to receive my prize-money least I should lose my chance of going to England.—I went with the Spanish prisoners to Spain; and came to Old-England with the English prisoners.—I cannot describe my joy when we were within sight of Portsmouth. But I was astonished when we landed to hear the inhabitants of that place curse and swear, and otherwise profane. I expected to find nothing but goodness, gentleness and meekness in this Christian Land, I then suffer'd great perplexities of mind.

I enquir'd if any serious Christian people resided there, the woman I made this enquiry of, answer'd me in the affirmative; and added that she was one of them.—I was heartily glad to hear her say so. I thought I could give her my whole heart: she kept a Public-House. I deposited with her all the money that I had not an immediate occasion for; as I thought it would be safer with her.—It was 25 guineas but 6 of them I desired her to lay out to the best advantage, to buy me some shirts, hat and some other necessaries. I made her a present of a very handsome large looking glass that I brought with me from Martinico, in order to recompence her for the trouble I had given her. I must do this woman the justice to acknowledge that she did lay out some little for my use, but the 19 guineas and part of the 6, with my watch, she would not return, but denied that I ever gave it her.

I soon perceived that I was got among bad people, who defrauded me of my money and watch; and that all my promis'd happiness was blasted, I had no friend but GOD and I pray'd to Him earnestly. I could scarcely believe it possible that the place where so many eminent Christians had lived and preached could abound with so much wickedness and deceit. I thought it worse than *Sodom* (considering the great advantages they have) I cryed like a child and that almost continually: at length GOD heard my prayers and rais'd me a friend indeed.

This publican had a brother who lived on Portsmouth-common, his wife was a very serious good woman.—When she heard of the treatment I had met with, she came and enquired into my real situation and was greatly troubled at the ill usage I had received, and took me home to her own house.—I began now to rejoice, and my prayer was turned into praise. She made use of all the arguments in her power to prevail on her who had wronged me, to return my watch and money, but it was to no purpose, as she had given me no receipt and I had nothing to show for it, I could not demand it.—My good friend was excessively angry with her and obliged her to give me back four guineas, which she said she gave me out of charity: Though in fact it was my own, and much more. She would have employed some rougher means to oblige her to give up my money, but I would not suffer her, let it go says I "My GOD is in heaven." Still I did not mind my loss in the least; all that grieved me was, that I had been disappointed in finding some Christian friends, with whom I hoped to enjoy a little sweet and comfortable society.

I thought the best method that I could take now, was to go to London, and find out Mr. Whitefield, who was the only living soul I knew in England, and get him to direct me to some way or other to procure a living without being troublesome to any Person.—I took leave of my Christian friend at Portsmouth, and went in the stage to London.—A creditable tradesman in the City, who went up with me in the stage, offer'd to show me the way to Mr. Whitefield's Tabernacle. Knowing that I was a perfect stranger, I thought it very kind, and accepted his offer; but he obliged me to give him half-a-crown for going with me, and likewise insisted on my giving him five shillings more for conducting me to Dr. Gifford's Meeting.

I began now to entertain a very different idea of the inhabitants of England than what I had figur'd to myself before I came amongst them.—Mr. Whitefield receiv'd me very friendly, was heartily glad to see me, and directed me to a proper place to board and lodge in Petticoat-Lane, till he could think of some way to settle me in, and paid for my lodging, and all my expences. The morning after I came to my new lodging, as I was at breakfast with the gentlewoman of the house, I heard the noise of some looms over our heads: I enquir'd what it was; she told me a person was weaving silk.—I express'd a great desire to see it, and ask'd if I might: She told me she would go up with me; she was sure I should be very welcome. She was as good as her word, and as soon as we enter'd the room, the person that was weaving look'd about, and smiled upon us, and I loved her from that moment.—She ask'd me many questions, and I in turn talk'd a great deal to her. I found she was a member of Mr. Allen's Meeting, and I begun to entertain a good opinion of her, though I was almost afraid to indulge this inclination, least she should prove like all the rest I had met with at Portsmouth, &c. and which had almost given me a dislike to all white women.—But after a short acquaintance I had the happiness to find she was very different, and quite sincere, and I was not without hope that she entertain'd some esteem for me. We often went together to hear Dr. Gifford, and as I had always a propensity to relieve every object in distress as far as I was able, I used to give to all that complain'd to me; sometimes half a guinea at a time, as I did not understand the real value of it.—This gracious, good woman took great pains to correct and advise me in that and many other respects.

After I had been in London about six weeks I was recommended to the notice of some of my late Master Mr. Freelandhouse's acquaintance, who had heard him speak frequently of me. I was much persuaded by them to go to Holland.—My Master lived there before he bought me, and used to speak of me so respectfully among his friends there, that it raised in them a curiosity to see me; particularly the Gentlemen engaged in the Ministry, who expressed a desire to hear my experience and examine me. I found that it was my good old Master's design that I should have gone if he had lived; for which reason I resolved upon going to Holland, and informed my dear friend Mr. Whitefield of my intention; he was much averse to my going at first, but after I gave him my reasons appeared very well satisfied. I likewise informed my Betty (the good woman that I have mentioned above) of my determination to go to Holland and I told her that I believed she was to be my Wife: that if it was the LORD's Will I desired it, but not else.—She made me very little answer, but has since told me, she did not think it at that time.

I embarked at Tower-wharf at four o'clock in the morning, and arriv'd at Amsterdam the next day by three o'clock in the afternoon. I had several letters of recommendation to my old master's friends, who receiv'd me very graciously. Indeed, one of the chief Ministers was particularly good to me; he kept me at his house a long while, and took great pleasure in asking questions, which I answer'd with delight, being always ready to say, *"Come unto me all ye that fear GOD, and I will tell what he hath done for my Soul."* I cannot but admire the footsteps of Providence; astonish'd that I should be so wonderfully preserved! Though the Grandson of a King, I have wanted bread, and should have been glad of the hardest crust I ever saw. I who, at home, was surrounded and guarded by slaves, so that no indifferent person might approach me, and clothed with gold, have been inhumanly threatened with death; and frequently wanted clothing to defend me from the inclemency of the weather; yet I never murmured, nor was I discontented.—I am willing, and even desirous to be counted as nothing, a stranger in the world, and a pilgrim here; for *"I know that my Redeemer liveth,"* and I'm thankful for every trial and trouble that I've met with, as I am not without hope that they have been all sanctified to me.

The Calvinist Ministers desired to hear my Experience from myself, which proposal I was very well pleased with: So I stood before 38 Ministers every Thursday for seven weeks together, and they were all very well satisfied, and persuaded I was what I pretended to be.—They wrote down my experience as I spoke it; and the LORD ALMIGHTY was with me at that time in a remarkable manner, and gave me words and enabled me to answer them; so great was his mercy to take me in hand a poor blind heathen.

At this time a very rich Merchant at AMSTERDAM offered to take me into his family in the capacity of his Butler, and I very willingly accepted it.—He was a gracious worthy Gentleman and very good to me.—He treated me more like a friend than a servant.—I tarried there a twelvemonth but was not thoroughly contented, I wanted to see my wife; (that is now) and for that reason I wished to return to *England*, I wrote to her once in my absence, but she did not answer my letter; and I must acknowledge if she had, it would have given me a less opinion of her.—My Master and Mistress persuaded me much not to leave them and likewise their two Sons who entertained a good opinion of me; and if I had found my Betty married on my arrival in ENGLAND, I should have returned to them again immediately.

My Lady purposed my marrying her maid; she was an agreeable young woman, had saved a good deal of money, but I could not fancy her, though she was willing to accept of me, but I told her my inclinations were engaged in ENGLAND, and I could think of no other Person.—On my return home, I found my Betty disengaged.—She had refused several offers in my absence, and told her sister that, she thought, if ever she married I was to be her husband.

Soon after I came home, I waited on Doctor Gifford who took me into his family and was exceedingly, good to me. The character of this pious worthy Gentleman is well known; my praise can be of no use or signification at all.—I hope I shall ever gratefully remember the many favours I have received from him.—Soon after I came to Doctor Gifford I expressed a desire to be admitted into their Church, and set down with them; they told me I must first be baptized; so I gave in my experience before the Church, with which they were very well satisfied, and I was baptized by Doctor Gifford with some others. I then made known my intentions of being married; but I found there were many objections against it because the person I had fixed on was poor. She was a widow, her husband had left her in debt, and with a child, so that they persuaded me against it out of real regard to me.—But I had promised and was resolved to have her; as I knew her to be a gracious woman, her poverty was no objection to me, as they had nothing else to say against her. When my friends found that they could not alter my opinion respecting her, they wrote to Mr. Allen, the Minister she attended, to persuade her to leave me; but he replied that he would not interfere at all, that we might do as we would. I was resolved that all my wife's little debt should be paid before we were married; so that I sold almost every thing I had and with all the money I could raise cleared all that she owed, and I never did any thing with a better will in all my Life, because I firmly believed that we should be very happy together, and so it prov'd, for she was given me from the LORD. And I have found her a blessed partner, and we have never repented, tho' we have gone through many great troubles and difficulties.

My wife got a very good living by weaving, and could do extremely well; but just at that time there was great disturbance among the weavers; so that I was afraid to let my wife work, least they should insist on my joining the rioters which I could not think of, and, possibly, if I had refused to do so they would have knock'd me on the head.—So that by these means my wife could get no employ, neither had I work enough to maintain my family. We had not yet been married a year before all these misfortunes overtook us.

Just at this time a gentleman, that seemed much concerned for us, advised me to go into Essex with him and promised to get me employed.—I accepted his kind proposal, and he spoke to a friend of his, a Quaker, a gentleman of large fortune, who resided a little way out of the town of *Colchester*, his name was *Handbarar*; he ordered his steward to set me to work. There were several employed in the same way with myself. I was very thankful and contented though my wages were but small.—I was allowed but eight pence a day, and found myself; but after I had been in this situation for a fortnight, my Master, being told that a Black was at work for him, had an inclination to see me. He was pleased to talk to me for some time, and at last enquired what wages I had; when I told him he declared, it was too little, and immediately ordered his Steward to let me have eighteen pence a day, which he constantly gave me after; and I then did extremely well.

I did not bring my wife with me: I came first alone and it was my design, if things answered according to our wishes, to send for her—I was now thinking to desire her to come to me when I receiv'd a letter to inform me she was just brought to bed and in want of many necessaries.—This news was a great trial to me and a fresh affliction: but my GOD, *faithful and abundant in mercy*, forsook me not in this trouble.—As I could not read *English*, I was obliged to apply to some one to read the letter I received, relative to my wife. I was directed by the good Providence of GOD to a worthy young gentleman, a Quaker, and friend of my Master.—I desired he would take the trouble to read my letter for me, which he readily comply'd with and was greatly moved and affected at the contents; insomuch that he said he would undertake to make a gathering for me, which he did and was the first to contribute to it himself. The money was sent that evening to LONDON by a person who happen'd to be going there: nor was this All the goodness that I experienced from these kind friends, for, as soon as my wife came about and was fit to travel, they sent for her to me, and were at the whole expence of her coming; so evidently has the love and mercy of GOD appeared through every trouble that ever I experienced. We went on very comfortably all the summer.—We lived in a little cottage near Mr. *Handbarrar's* House; but when the winter came on I was discharged, as he had no further occasion for me. And now the prospect began to darken upon us again. We thought it most adviseable to move our habitation a little nearer to the Town, as the house we lived in was very cold, and wet, and ready to tumble down.

The boundless goodness of GOD to me has been so very great, that with the most humble gratitude I desire to prostrate myself before Him; for I have been wonderfully supported in every affliction. My GOD never left me. I perceived light still through the thickest darkness.

My dear wife and I were now both unemployed, we could get nothing to do. The winter prov'd remarkably severe, and we were reduc'd to the greatest distress imaginable.—I was always very shy of asking for any thing; I could never beg; neither did I chuse to make known our wants to any person, for fear of offending as we were entire strangers; but our last bit of bread was gone, and I was obliged to think of something to do for our support.—I did not mind for myself at all; but to see my dear wife and children in want pierc'd me to the heart.—I now blam'd myself for bringing her from London, as doubtless had we continued there we might have found friends to keep us from starving. The snow was at this season remarkably deep; so that we could see no prospect of being relieved. In this melancholy situation, not knowing what step to pursue, I resolved to make my case known to a Gentleman's Gardiner that lived near us, and entreat him to employ me: but when I came to him, my courage failed me, and I was ashamed to make known our real situation.—I endeavoured all I could to prevail on him to set me to work, but to no purpose: he assur'd me it was not in his power: but just as I was about to leave him, he asked me if I would accept of some Carrots? I took them with great thankfulness and carried them home: he gave me four, they were very large and fine.—We had nothing to make fire with, so consequently could not boil them: But was glad to have them to eat *raw*. Our youngest child was quite an infant; so that my wife was obliged to chew it, and fed her in that manner for several days.—We allowed ourselves but one every day, least they should not last 'till we could get some other supply. I was unwilling to eat at all myself; nor would I take any the last day that we continued in this situation, as I could not bear the thought that my dear wife and children would be in want of every means of support. We lived in this manner, 'till our carrots were all gone: then my Wife began to lament because of our poor babies: but I comforted her all I could; still hoping, and believing that *my* GOD would not let us die: but that it would please Him to relieve us, which *He* did by almost a Miracle.

We went to bed, as usual, before it was quite dark, (as we had neither fire nor candle) but had not been there long before some person knocked at the door & enquir'd if *James Albert* lived there? I answer'd in the affirmative, and rose immediately; as soon as I open'd the door I found it was the servant of an eminent Attorney who resided at *Colchester*.—He ask'd me how it was with me? if I was not almost starv'd? I burst out a crying, and told him I was indeed. He said his master suppos'd so, and that he wanted to speak with me, and I must return with him. This Gentleman's name was *Danniel*, he was a sincere, good Christian. He used to stand and talk with me frequently when I work'd in the road for Mr. *Handbarrar*, and would have employed me himself, if I had wanted work.—When I came to his house he told me that he had thought a good deal about me of late, and was apprehensive that I must be in want, and could not be satisfied till he sent to enquire after me. I made known my distress to him, at which he was greatly affected; and generously gave me a guinea; and promis'd to be kind to me in future. I could not help exclaiming. *O the boundless mercies of my God!* I pray'd unto Him, and He has heard me; I trusted in Him and He has preserv'd me: where shall I begin to praise Him, or how shall I love Him enough?

I went immediately and bought some bread and cheese and coal and carried it home. My dear wife was rejoiced to see me return with something to eat. She instantly got up and dressed our Babies, while I made a fire, and the first Nobility in the land never made a more comfortable meal.—We did not forget to thank the LORD for all his goodness to us.—Soon after this, as the spring came on, Mr. Peter *Daniel* employed me in helping to pull down a house, and rebuilding it. I had then very good work, and full employ: he sent for my wife, and children to *Colchester*, and provided us a house where we lived very comfortably.—I hope I shall always gratefully acknowledge his kindness to myself and family. I worked at this house for more than a year, till it was finished; and after that I was employed by several successively, and was never so happy as when I had something to do; but perceiving the winter coming on, and work rather slack, I was apprehensive that we should again be in want or become troublesome to our friends.

I had at this time an offer made me of going to *Norwich* and having constant employ.—My wife seemed pleased with this proposal, as she supposed she might get work there in the weaving-manufactory, being the business she was brought up to, and more likely to succeed there than any other place; and we thought as we had an opportunity of moving to a Town where we could both be employ'd it was most adviseable to do so; and that probably we might settle there for our lives.—When this step was resolv'd on, I went first alone to see how it would answer; which I very much repented after, for it was not in my power immediately to send my wife any supply, as I fell into the hands of a Master that was neither kind nor considerate; and she was reduced to great distress, so that she was oblig'd to sell the few goods that we had, and when I sent for her was under the disagreeable necessity of parting with our bed.

The Life of James Albert Ukawsaw Gronniosaw

When she came to *Norwich* I hired a room ready furnished.—I experienced a great deal of difference in the carriage of my Master from what I had been accustomed to from some of my other Masters. He was very irregular in his payments to me.—My wife hired a loom and wove all the leisure time she had and we began to do very well, till we were overtaken by fresh misfortunes. Our three poor children fell ill of the small pox; this was a great trial to us; but still I was persuaded in myself we should not be forsaken.—And I did all in my power to keep my dear partner's spirits from sinking. Her whole attention now was taken up with the children as she could mind nothing else, and all I could get was but little to support a family in such a situation, beside paying for the hire of our room, which I was obliged to omit doing for several weeks: but the woman to whom we were indebted would not excuse us, tho' I promised she should have the very first money we could get after my children came about, but she would not be satisfied and had the cruelty to threaten us that if we did not pay her immediately she would turn us all into the street.

The apprehension of this plunged me in the deepest distress, considering the situation of my poor babies: if they had been in health I should have been less sensible of this misfortune. But My GOD, *still faithful to his promise*, raised me a friend. Mr. Henry Gurdney, a Quaker, a gracious gentleman heard of our distress, he sent a servant of his own to the woman we hired the room of, paid our rent, and bought all the goods with my wife's loom and gave it us all.

Some other gentlemen, hearing of his design, were pleased to assist him in these generous acts, for which we never can be thankful enough; after this my children soon came about; we began to do pretty well again; my dear wife work'd hard and constant when she could get work, but it was upon a disagreeable footing as her employ was so uncertain, sometimes she could get nothing to do and at other times when the weavers of *Norwich* had orders from London they were so excessively hurried, that the people they employ'd were often oblig'd to work on the *Sabbath-day*; but this my wife would never do, and it was matter of uneasiness to us that we could not get our living in a regular manner, though we were both diligent, industrious, and willing to work. I was far from being happy in my Master, he did not use me well. I could scarcely ever get my money from him; but I continued patient 'till it pleased GOD to alter my situation.

My worthy friend Mr. Gurdney advised me to follow the employ of chopping chaff, and bought me an instrument for that purpose. There were but few people in the town that made this their business beside myself; so that I did very well indeed and we became easy and happy.—But we did not continue long in this comfortable state: Many of the inferior people were envious and ill-natur'd and set up the same employ and work'd under price on purpose to get my business from me, and they succeeded so well that I could hardly get any thing to do, and became again unfortunate: Nor did this misfortune come alone, for just at this time we lost one of our little girls who died of a fever; this circumstance occasion'd us new troubles, for the Baptist Minister refused to bury her because we were not their members. The Parson of the parish denied us because she had never been baptized. I applied to the Quakers, but met with no success; this was one of the greatest trials I ever met with, as we did not know what to do with our poor baby.—At length I resolv'd to dig a grave in the garden behind the house, and bury her there; when the Parson of the parish sent for me to tell me he would bury the child, but did not chuse to read the burial service over her. I told him I did not mind whether he would or not, as the child could not hear it.

We met with a great deal of ill treatment after this, and found it very difficult to live.—We could scarcely get work to do, and were obliged to pawn our cloaths. We were ready to sink under our troubles.—When I purposed to my wife to go to *Kidderminster* and try if we could do there. I had always an inclination for that place, and now more than ever as I had heard *Mr. Fawcet* mentioned in the most respectful manner, as a pious worthy Gentleman; and I had seen his name in a favourite book of mine, Baxter's *Saints everlasting rest*, and as the Manufactory of *Kidderminster* seemed to promise my wife some employment, she readily came into my way of thinking.

I left her once more, and set out for *Kidderminster*, in order to judge if the situation would suit us.—As soon as I came there I waited immediately on *Mr. Fawcet*, who was pleased to receive me very kindly and recommended me to *Mr. Watson* who employed me in twisting silk and worsted together. I continued here about a fortnight, and when I thought it would answer our expectation, I returned to *Norwich* to fetch my wife; she was then near her time, and too much indisposed. So we were obliged to tarry until she was brought to bed, and as soon as she could conveniently travel we came to *Kidderminster*, but we brought nothing with us as we were obliged to sell all we had to pay our debts and the expences of my wife's illness, &c.

Such is our situation at present.—My wife, by hard labor at the loom, does every thing that can be expected from her towards the maintenance of our family; and God is pleased to incline the hearts of his People at times to yield us their charitable assistance; being myself through age and infirmity able to contribute but little to their support. As Pilgrims, and very poor Pilgrims, we are travelling through many difficulties towards our HEAVENLY HOME, and waiting patiently for his gracious call, when the LORD shall deliver us out of the evils of this present world and bring us to the EVERLASTING GLORIES of the world to come.—To HIM be PRAISE for EVER and EVER, AMEN.

FINIS.

Lightning Source UK Ltd.
Milton Keynes UK
UKOW02f0900290316

271079UK00001B/258/P

9 781409 974703